OSCAR POLLYS

STOP COMPARING YOURSELF

The Essential Guide on Loving and Being Confident in Yourself, Learn How to Stop Caring What Other People Think Of You and Become Confident in Yourself

Descrierea CIP a Bibliotecii Naționale a României
OSCAR POLLYS
STOP COMPARING YOURSELF. The Essential Guide on Loving and Being Confident in Yourself, Learn How to Stop Caring What Other People Think Of You and Become Confident in Yourself / Oscar Pollys. – Bucharest: Editura My Ebook, 2020
ISBN 978-606-983-600-2

OSCAR POLLYS

STOP COMPARING YOURSELF

The Essential Guide on Loving and Being Confident in Yourself, Learn How to Stop Caring What Other People Think Of You and Become Confident in Yourself

My Ebook Publishing House
Bucharest, 2020

TABLE OF CONTENT

Introduction

Everybody compares themselves to other people and have been doing this since they were a child. It is a natural thing for people to do because it provides a frame of reference for who they are and where they are in life.

The problem is that most comparisons are negative and based on insecurities and fear. This can lead to a person becoming very bitter about another individual and even angry. Negative comparisons like these often damage a person's self worth because they believe that they are not good enough.

Some people use comparisons to boost their ego and to validate that they are great. This can often backfire and when it does the person is left feeling angry and bitter and their self esteem takes a big hit. People make validation comparisons for quick ego boosts but these are not foolproof by any means.

There are a lot of people that idolize others and end up being overly dependent on them. They dedicate their lives to making these people happy and can only be happy themselves if they feel they have done enough. In this situation the person being idolized has too much control of the other person.

Not all comparisons are bad as you will learn in this guide. You can use comparisons to improve your life and you will learn exactly how to do this here. The aim of this guide is to move you away from negative comparisons and start using positive comparisons to make your life better.

Why we compare ourselves to others

It is a natural thing for human beings to compare themselves to others. We all do it and have done since an early age. But the issue really is about how those comparisons make you feel. If they empower you and spur you on to greater things then comparisons are very useful.

But if when you are comparing yourself with others you feel unworthy and depressed then this is where you need to change your approach. In this book you will learn exactly how to stop comparing yourself to others to prevent these feelings of worthlessness and also how you can actually benefit from a comparison.

Once you have mastered how to use comparisons in a good way you will find that you can automatically brush off any negative comparisons. It will not bother you that someone has something you don't. You will be focused on improving yourself and your own life.

Take a good look at yourself

We have the capability to take a good look at ourselves and work out who we really are. This is one of those things that sets human beings apart from the rest of the animal kingdom. At any time we can go into deep thought about our life's mission. We can become inspired to be the very best that we can be rather than just drift along in life.

So what is the best way to really evaluate yourself? The answer is that you need to compare yourself to others! That might sound counterintuitive but it is true. It is no use comparing yourself to your pet dog or cat. They are different species and will have few qualities that will want to aspire to.

The trick is to make the comparisons benefit you. Most people have standards in their heads that have not come from within but are externally influenced. Think about the girl who wants to lose a few pounds because she wants to look like the model on the cover of a magazine. Or the boy going to the gym because he wants those six pack abs he has seen in the movies.

The trouble with these kinds of comparisons is that they have not come from within you. Instead of developing your own standards for beauty you have let the external world dictate that to you.

The Festinger Research

Leon Festinger, a social psychologist, started to look into the reasons that we compare ourselves to others back in the 1950's. After a lot of research and different studies he came to the conclusion that people compared themselves to others for 2 main reasons:

1. As a way to reduce uncertainty in their own life
2. To learn how they should define how they should be

Festinger called this "social comparison theory" and it was a significant breakthrough in human psychology. The real breakthrough was how he uncovered that people were incapable of defining themselves independently or intrinsically. They have to make comparisons with others to achieve this.

The bottom line is that to define yourself you need to compare yourself with other people. He also made the important

11

discovery that if there is a big difference in ability or opinion between two people that there was much less chance that a comparison would occur.

So here is an important takeaway from Festinger's work:

The more we think that a person is similar to us (for whatever important reasons) the more likely we are to want to compare with them.

Here is a common example. At work you are far more likely to compare yourself to someone who works on your team (an equal) than you are with the owner of the business or the CEO. If you play amateur soccer then you will compare yourself to other players in your league much more than you will to Lionel Messi.

The difference between an amateur soccer player and Lionel Messi is vast but the difference between another amateur player is probably not that much. It is a lot more realistic for you to achieve the level of the other amateur player than it is to emulate Messi.

It was also discovered by Festinger that when a person stops comparing themselves with another person where they experience pain from not being like them that they are highly likely to be hostile with this person.

When you stop comparing yourself to another person that makes you feel down then the way that most people deal with this is to "tear down" their feelings towards that individual. Often you will substitute another emotion such as anger to replace the negative experiences of the comparison.

Can you relate to this?

Have you ever stopped comparing yourself to another person because this was too painful for you and then turned against the individual? If you did this then you are certainly not alone as it is a very common practice.

The final conclusion from Festinger's work was that if we feel that a person or group of people are very important then we will exert a lot of pressure on ourselves to try and conform to the opinions and abilities of this person or group.

So for example if you have joined a power spin class at your gym you could feel that it is far more important for you to put in the maximum effort there than you would if you were to meet some cyclists on the road. You see the spin club as an elite group that you need to aspire to whereas the cyclists on the road hold little importance for you.

In fact the spin class is so important to you that you pay your hard earned money to be part of it – and so does everyone else in the class!

Why you compare yourself to others

At this stage you may be thinking that all that we have discussed so far is obvious and you would be right. But why do you keep acting in this way and experiencing negative emotions when comparing yourself to someone else doesn't work out well?

Well you do this for two main reasons:

1. You want to know just how good you are

2. You want to improve yourself

These reasons are extremely important and later we will discuss how you can make comparisons that are healthy for you rather than those that are not.

In the next chapter we will discuss why comparing yourself to others can be a bad thing to do…

The Dangers Of Comparing Yourself To Others

Insecurity and fear are the main reasons that we compare ourselves to others. This can lead to a lot of problems in our life which we will explain in detail in the next chapter. What are we afraid of? Well most people believe that if other people really knew who we were then they wouldn't like us, let alone love us.

The insecurity part is our failure to see the true value that we have to offer. We can either undervalue ourselves or overvalue ourselves. If you think that you have very little value as a person then craving the approval of others is very likely. In a situation where you think you are more valuable than you really are then you can often use others to validate this.

We Focus on the wrong things

When we reach adulthood we are far more likely to become aware of our own shortcomings and thoughts about ourselves. Once this happen they become a major focus for us. All around us are social pressures to grow hair if we are balding, get six pack abs if we are looking flabby and make our teeth whiter for example.

Being bombarded with these messages each day often brings a lot of pain to people and really doesn't do much to make a positive change in our lives. Our self esteem takes a nose dive when we are confronted with these things so we just feel like giving up and staying the way we are.

People tend to live with a number of different paradoxes. The fact is that we are good enough but we can always get better. There are actually advantages to comparing yourself to others if you do it right and we will cover this in a later chapter. You have to consider this question when you compare yourself to others:

Is your comparison with others based on insecurity and fear or is it because you want to improve yourself?

Let's take a look at each of these in turn:

Comparing yourself to others based on Insecurity and Fear

So many people do this but it is not a place that you want to be. This is likely to do you a lot more harm than good. A few years ago you might have heard this called "coveting what others have".

How do you feel about the following scenarios?

- Someone that you work with and know very well gets promoted before you do - do you feel angry about this?
- Your neighbor has a better car than you – does this make you feel jealous?
- An old friend has developed a specific talent which has enabled them to set up their own business and make a lot of money – do you feel resentful about this?

If you feel very strongly that you deserve more out of life than you are currently getting then this can drive fear within you that you are just not good enough. Why should a person that joined your team after you did get promoted before you? Why should an old friend that you went to school with who was no brighter than you now be making much more money than you?

When you have strong feelings like this then it is very easy to become bitter and feel discontented. This can easily lead you into a "pity spiral" where you start to feel sorry for yourself often and lose your passion for life.

Another danger of being bitter is you can start to think bad things about the person who seemingly has more than you do. You know them very well and they just don't deserve to be making more money or having a nicer car than you.

If bitterness really gets a hold in your life then your anger levels will rise significantly. You can start thinking evil thoughts like wishing harm on another person that has more money than you or hoping that someone steals your neighbor's car for example.

Living a life centered around insecurity and fear leads to hopelessness and very little joy. You will become obsessed with the fact that you are simply not good enough so what is the point of it all?

There are examples of this insecurity and fear all around us. You probably know someone who is divorced that totally despises the fact that their ex is now happy with a new person.

Instead of focusing on finding the right person to make them happy they cling on to the past and live in resentment.

People that live this way often feel that they will never be good enough and end up just surviving rather than growing and leading a fulfilling life. If you do not escape this kind of bitterness then you will never truly be happy.

Comparing yourself to others based on the desire to Improve

Sometimes you just watch someone else performing and just find it completely awe inspiring. This happens a lot on sport where a budding young sports star who has to work tirelessly to improve their performance watches an experienced pro who just seems to make it all look effortless.

You can use this kind of inspiration to motivate yourself. Seeing a sports star do the things that you want to do effortlessly is usually down to years of experience. But it can really spur you on to work harder and achieve the skillset that this person has. If they can do it you can do it too.

Of course there is another side to this coin. And that is becoming resentful and bitter towards the sports star or whoever you are in awe of. You need to learn to use a comparison positively rather than negatively. Don't fall into bitterness and resentment. Go for inspiration instead.

You Let others Drive your Behavior

Another downside of comparing yourself to others for the wrong reasons is that you put your life in their hands. You need to be on par with them or better to feel happy and contented. This is a very undesirable situation.

Here is a reality check for you:

There are always going to be people that are better at some things than you!

And on the flip side of the coin...

You are going to be better than them at other things!

In a later chapters we will show you how you can focus on the most important person in the world – YOU. We will show you how to concentrate all of your thoughts on loving yourself more, raising your self esteem and boosting your self confidence.

In the next chapter we will look at how you can choose to make healthy comparisons with others that will help you...

How To Make
Healthy Comparisons

You have learned a lot so far. You now know why we make comparisons with others and the dangers of making the wrong type of comparisons. In this chapter we will discuss how you can make comparisons with others that are actually beneficial to you.

It Starts with Intention

If you want to make healthy comparisons then you need intent. You are consciously choosing to compare yourself to someone else for a positive reason. It has nothing to do with envy or any other negative emotion that will make you feel terrible.

You can choose a person currently living or dead for your healthy comparison. As long as there is information about them that will help you to change the way that you think and behave for the better then is doesn't matter.

Your intention is always to learn from these people so that you can make better decisions in life. As you move from one situation to another you can think to yourself "how would the person that I am comparing myself to handle this situation?" If you really know a lot about them then you should get the answer you are looking for.

You are not limited to just making healthy comparisons with just one person. Nobody is good at everything so you can have a number of people that you compare yourself to in different situations. It all depends where you want to be as a person.

Know what is going on around you

The second step to making healthy comparisons of others is to listen to and watch what is going on around you. Are there politicians or other intellectuals that you will not pay any attention to because you do not agree with their point of view? Or maybe you do not like a particular sports star who is at the top of their game so you ignore them?

We do not recommend that you do this! Forget about any biases that you have and be prepared to learn from these people. Listen to what they have to say and watch what they do. It doesn't matter if you agree with them or not they can teach you some valuable lessons.

Look for leaders in your field and listen intently to them and watch how they behave. It doesn't matter if you agree with their philosophy or not because you can use this to determine some of the things that you do not want to do. And of course you might learn some good things from them too. You will always win by doing this.

Become an Avid Reader

Do you read regularly? This doesn't have to mean buying books as there are plenty of inspiring and helpful online resources that you can learn from. When was the last time that you read an inspirational blog post about a topic of interest that could help you to improve your life?

Today you can find videos about all kinds of subject that you can learn from. A lot of people prefer to watch a video and make some important notes than read a lot of text. That's fine – just do what works for you.

Another great way to improve your life through healthy comparison is to take training courses. There are tons of free training courses online as well as paid courses so identify the training that you need and go find it. An informative and inspiring training course can really give you a boost so make a commitment to find your course today.

Forget about being better than others

A lot of people tend to compare themselves to others to boost their egos. When they do this they get the satisfaction of seeing themselves more favorably. If you do this then we recommend that you stop this practice right now.

Why?

Because this will not help you to grow. It will give you a temporary feeling of satisfaction at someone else's expense. You are not trying to improve yourself by making these kinds of comparisons. It just gives your self esteem a bit of a lift – but not in the right way.

When you make comparisons in this negative way then it is very easy to build up a distorted picture of yourself. There has been a lot of research in this area that shows that people that do this tend to prioritize feedback that makes them look good and more desirable.

The same people are not interested in any feedback that identifies their weaknesses or their undesirability. By avoiding this kind of reality your brain is really playing a trick on you. It is telling you that everything is good when really it isn't.

Comparing yourself to others to find out just how good you are is a road to disaster. It will end up making you very miserable because you may not always get the results that you want. Sure comparing yourself to someone that you know is weaker than you can give you a feeling of superiority, but it can also uncover some of your vulnerabilities that you don't want to know about.

When this happens you are likely to feel shame or even anger. We call this comparison process "self enhancement" and it is a very dangerous game to play. Let's say that you consider yourself to be the best player of a certain video game. You consistently get very high scores and feel invincible.

You meet a new person who says that they have never played the game before. They are willing to try to play against you and you are feeling very confident. The game commences and this person beats you. How do you feel? You are certainly going to feel some form of shame. Then anger can creep in and you can end up throwing the game controller to the floor.

Don't hold on to your Self View

We all have a view about ourselves and how we think we stack up against the rest. Then we use this in our comparisons to gauge whether we are smarter or as smart as someone else, whether we are better looking or as good looking, more talented or as talented etc.

You have formed this self view of yourself over many years and it all started in your childhood. The opinions that you have formed about yourself are an essential part of your self esteem. Your "self view" is absolutely critical to you. It defines the way that you see the world and helps you to make sense of everything.

We will do almost anything to protect our self view. But the problem is that it can make your comparisons with others very negative. These pre-existing opinions you have of yourself are always working when you make comparisons. It is the reason that you make the comparisons in the first place.

So the tendency is for you to make a lot of comparisons so that you can confirm your self view. If you believe that you are a great public speaker then you will look for ways to verify this. What you don't want to hear is feedback that you still need to sharpen your skills.

But what if you could be accepting of this kind of feedback? What if you have the belief that you can always learn something new and that you are not the finished item? This may be extremely difficult for you to take on board at first, but it will help you to make much healthier comparisons.

- In the next chapter we will look at ways that you can take small steps to make big changes when it comes to comparing yourself to others…

Small Steps
For Big Changes

To really get the best out of your comparisons with others you need to have strong self esteem. If you are experiencing negative reactions from a lot of your comparisons then your self esteem is going to need some work.

Changing the way that you use comparisons with others is going to take effort and persistence. It is not going to happen overnight and there is no magic formula. But if you follow the advice in this book and take small steps every day then you will get there and improve your life no end.

Compare Yourself with Yourself

As most people mature they tend to naturally develop a stronger sense of who they are and compare themselves with others a lot less because they don't need to. But usually this is not a perfect scenario as there will still be some areas that they feel the need to make comparisons about.

What we are asking you to do is to make a commitment to compare yourself with yourself and forget about others. What does this mean? Well it is all about making the decision that you are just going to please yourself and that you will be the judge of what is good and what is not.

When you make this transformation you will empower yourself and it will motivate you to achieve more and will also be therapeutic. You are not trying to compete with everyone else and you can set yourself realistic and attainable goals that really matter to you.

It is best to treat this transformation as a journey. Every day you will take small steps and when you achieve victories on your journey then you will celebrate them. By making this change it doesn't mean that you cut off comparing yourself with others to improve yourself – far from it.

Once you decide to be yourself then everything changes. You no longer have seek the approval of others to be happy. In today's world there are many influences that are seeking to turn you into something that you are not. It is a major achievement to be yourself.

Giving your Consent to Feel Inferior

Eleanor Roosevelt said "no one can make you feel inferior without your consent". This is very true. By comparing yourself to others in a negative way you are giving your consent to feel negatively about the outcome. You are violating yourself by making these comparisons, but you chose to do this so have provided your consent.

So give yourself the consent to be the "best you" that you can be instead. Set your own agenda and take responsibility for your life. Tackle any challenges that you face head on and revel in the personal victories that you experience.

Just accept the fact that there will always be people that are better than you at something and conversely you will be better at something else than they are. At the end of the day it really doesn't matter. Planning your self journey and focusing on making the progress that you want to achieve is all that matters.

Change your biggest Idol to you

We all have idols in life, people that we admire and look up to. There is nothing wrong with this if you learn from these people to improve yourself. What we want you to do here is make your biggest idol yourself. Not just who you are today but the person that you have the potential to be.

Strive to become a role model for yourself. Stop dwelling in the past and focus on today and the future. It doesn't matter what happened to you in the past. What you couldn't do yesterday you can do today and tomorrow.

Believe that other people cannot judge you properly because they have no idea what your life journey is all about. Forget about what others are doing and make your life a whole lot easier. The important thing is to keep doing you.

Focus on your own Progress

If you have a goal to lose 20 pounds and are just starting out on this journey there is no point comparing yourself to someone that has the same aim but is well into their journey if this is going to make you feel depressed. It is a good thing to do if it will inspire you to make a great start and keep going.

You need to assess what works the best for you. We are all different and what motivates and inspires you can be totally different to everyone else. Never wish that you had someone else's life. A lot of people do this and it just drives them into a negative spiral. Take responsibility and just focus on your own journey.

Each minute that you spend wishing you had someone else's life is a minute of your own life that you have truly wasted. Don't waste any of your precious time on this. Take ownership of your life and live it to its fullest potential.

Define Success your way

You may not realize this but you have already achieved a lot in your life. A lot of people define success as what they have and overlook the fact they have had to overcome a lot of challenges in their lives.

There is a lot of power in taking a look back at the things that you have overcome in your life. This will give you great perspective on just how far you have come and how much you have grown.

When you were younger you probably worried a lot about a number of things in life:

- Will I make good money?
- Will I find my ideal partner in life?
- Will I have the things that I really want?
- Will I be able to drive a car and have the freedom to go wherever I want?

There are many other examples. Did you ever worry about these kinds of things? Of course you did so think back to how you overcame them and shaped your life to what it is today. You did it your way so be very proud of that.

Resist the temptation to try and achieve the same thing as somebody else. Set your own goals and do things your way. We would always recommend that you learn from others that have achieved what you want to inspire you. But don't just copy other people.

Once you have set your goals then focus on them and don't be distracted. Don't subscribe to the view that the "grass is greener someplace else". In the world of make money online there are new courses available every day. Quite often there is more than one new method available each day.

The creators of these new methods will sell you on the grass is greener approach. They will tell you that what you are doing now is not the best way to go and that their way is better. This is known as the "shiny object syndrome". Usually the only people that do well from this are the people that create these new products.

Just because a particular method worked well for someone else does not mean that it will work well for you. So if making money online is one of your goals then choose one method to do this and forget about everything else. If this method doesn't work out as you want it to then you can look around for another.

We are not saying that you shouldn't learn from others here. If you go down a particular path to achieve a goal then we absolutely encourage you to get the right training and use the best tools for the job. What we are saying is that you should focus on one thing before you move on to another.

In the next chapter we will discuss how you can learn to love yourself more so that you do not need be over dependent on what others think about you...

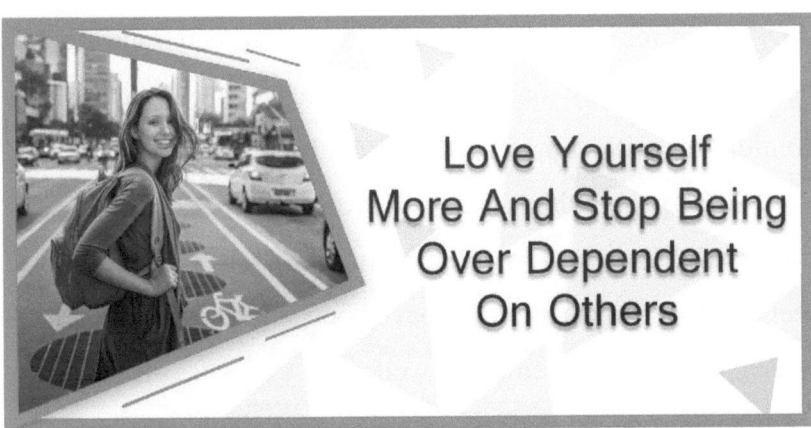

Love Yourself More And Stop Being Over Dependent On Others

We all want to be loved. This is a natural thing. We want to receive love from others and give them love back. The problem is that some people are so focused on pleasing the people around them that they forget to love themselves. Many people believe that they have to stay in a toxic relationship with someone because it is the right thing to do.

If you are in this situation then there is something very important that you need to know:

You can never truly love someone else until you love yourself.

If you rely on others for self validation then your life will never be a happy one. It is essential that you are totally comfortable with yourself and that you have strong self love.

Some people think that self love is a very selfish thing and this is why they tend to avoid it. It is not selfish. You need to feel confident in yourself and have good self esteem if you want to be happy and help others as well.

The stronger your self love the more likely you are to be happy. And you deserve to be happy! Having strong self love has nothing to do with ego. It is something that you develop from within. Developing a deep and genuine love for yourself is something that you must do.

Stop being Overly Dependent on others

The first thing to say here is that having a dependency on someone else is not a sign of weakness. If you are in a loving relationship then you will be dependent on your partner for a number of things. This is a healthy situation. What we are talking about here is over dependence.

You need to strike the right balance when it comes to dependency. We all need support, validation and encouragement from others in our life. Often you will grow stronger from these experiences in your life. You have the power to give back and help those that you love grow as well.

What you want to avoid at all costs is over dependency. If you are over dependent on others then it can be very difficult for you to realize your own independence. This can easily spiral out of control to the point where you are obsessing about what another person thinks and feels about you.

If you spend all of your time and energy trying to please others then it is very easy to lose sight of yourself. This can make you feel inadequate and empty and even make you feel that you are not real.

Over dependence can come from a variety of places. Your childhood can have a major influence here. Maybe you had a hard time at school or had issues with your parents. The bottom line is that it doesn't matter where your tendency for over dependency came from you can stop this by loving yourself more.

So here are the steps that you can take to love yourself more and free yourself from over dependence with others:

1. It comes from Within

If you are low on self love and rely too much on others then realize that the actions that you are taking to strengthen your over dependency all come from within. You hold beliefs that are driving you to perform these actions. The good news is that you can identify these beliefs and change them.

So if you are in an over dependent situation then start noting down how many times you seeking approval from others and what you do and say. Start a journal and write these things down. You need to know what you are up against before you can effectively tackle the problem.

2. Write and use Affirmations every day

It is great to receive praise from others but if you really want to improve your self love then you need to pay yourself compliments on a regular basis. This is the best way to develop authentic self love.

It is easy to write affirmations that provide these compliments. When you write them you can tell yourself that you are a great person who has a lot to offer the world. They are a great way to reinforce the strengths that you have and the goodness within you. You don't need approval from anyone else to write and read your affirmations.

Affirmations provide an easy and gentle way to get you firmly on the path of self love. They will help to improve your self esteem and develop truly fearless self love. How you use your affirmations is up to you. Some people like to read them out loud while others like to say them in their head.

The method that you use doesn't matter. Using your affirmations consistently does. So commit to reading your affirmations twice a day. Once when you get up in the morning and again before you retire at night.

3. Take Control of Negative Self Talk

If you are constantly seeking the approval of others you will have a lot of negative self talk going on in your head. This can be very destructive and you need to work on minimizing this as much as you can. You do not want to become a prisoner of your own mind. It is easier than you think to break free from negative self talk.

You need to identify when you are making harmful statements in your head and neutralize these thoughts with positive thoughts. Telling yourself that you are a failure all of the time or not good enough is very destructive. It is the antithesis of self love.

Reading your affirmations twice a day is a great way to start your authentic self love journey. But if you have a tendency to self criticize often then you can easily undo all of the good work that the affirmations can do for you.

So the first step to defeating negative self talk is to spot when you are doing it. An effective way to neutralize a negative thought is to replace it with a positive one. So if you think "I can't do this" then replace this with "I can do anything".

It is going to take you time and effort to replace your negative thinking with positive thinking but it is certainly worth it. Once you become a master at doing this then your life will become a lot more positive as a result.

4. Challenge External Expectations

In the days before the Internet people had to cope with social expectations from family and friends, work colleagues and other people that had influence in their lives. Now we are constantly exposed to different types of expectations through social media as well.

Sometimes these social influences can have a positive impact on your life but a lot of the time the impact is negative. We do not have the right body shape or wear the right clothes or drive the right car. The list of these expectations goes on and on.

Reacting to these external expectations is no different to seeking the approval of others and being overly dependent. It is a slippery slope that you want to avoid. The best way to tackle this is to seek approval from yourself rather than an external influence. Decide on what you truly value in life and stick with this. Don't be swayed by anyone or anything else.

5. Be Grateful

When you are grateful for what you have in your life you will shift your thoughts away from negativity. We recommend that you practice gratitude on a daily basis as it will help you to focus on the positive things in your life.

By being grateful each day you will begin to break down the barriers to loving yourself more. If you have never done this before then you may feel uncomfortable about doing it. There really isn't anything to worry about and if you follow the steps below you will find it very easy to do.

At the start of each day write down 3 things that you are grateful for. These can be literally anything from the fact that you are healthy and have life to the relationships that you have. As you write each of these down think about how you feel about them. After a few days of doing this you should notice an increase in your happiness and thankfulness.

To really help you with your self love it is a good idea to add a positive attribute about yourself each day. For example you could write "I am really grateful that I have the courage to overcome problems in my life". Even better quote a specific problem that you have overcome.

6. Identify your Strengths

Focusing on your strengths is a powerful way to improve your self love and to lessen your reliance on others. You might be thinking right now that you have no strengths which is why you are in this situation. But this is never the case.

If you are someone that is easily influenced by others then you may find that you have worked to develop skills that really didn't suit you in the past. Perhaps someone with influence in your life encouraged you to learn a foreign language which was convenient for them. But this was not something that you really wanted to do.

Think about the values that you hold. What do you really want out of life? We all have our own unique set of desires. What have you done in the past that is a strength? Do you keep going when others give up? Are you a natural with children? Think about this carefully and write a list of your strengths.

We recommend that you use a journal to record your life transformation. So write your strengths down in your journal under the heading "This is what I am good at" and then create a heading on the next page "This is what I am going to be good at" which will be the strengths that you want to develop in the future.

The strengths that you want to develop are what you want and not anyone else. Forget about others when you write this list. It is all about you. Don't put up any barriers when you are creating this list. Tell yourself that you can do anything and that you can always find a way.

7. Smile

Here is something that is really easy to do. Smiling often is a great step to take in your journey to self love. Did you know that when you smile you will change your emotional state immediately? No matter how bad things seem to be stand up and smile! You will feel so much better for doing this.

Smiling creates a chemical reaction in your brain designed to improve your mood. So make it a routine to stand in front of a mirror and smile. This should certainly make you feel good as your body releases serotonin and dopamine when you smile.

Make smiling regularly each day part of your self love journey. Smiling is not going to fix all of your problems but it sure is a great place to start. It will give you a lift that you can build upon to help you achieve the things that you want to do throughout the day.

8. Determine your Boundaries

If you don't have any boundaries set up then others will tend to treat you just as they want. On your journey to self love you need to set up boundaries with the rules that people need to observe on how to treat you.

It is all about creating a healthy relationship with others and with yourself. Your boundaries specify what you will allow in your life and what you won't. There are emotional and physical elements to boundaries and at the end of the day your boundaries are there to keep you safe.

After you have established your boundaries and communicated them to others then it is really important that you hold firm with them. If people attempt to violate your boundaries then you need to let them know in no uncertain terms.

As an example of a boundary you could set imagine that you spend too much time on social media. So you decide on a boundary that will limit the amount of time you spend on social media each day. This is excellent for self control and self discipline and will help to improve your self worth.

As you create these healthy boundaries for yourself and stick to them you will find that your self love will grow as a result. So take the time out to think about the personal boundaries that you want to set and that you want others to respect. Record these in your journal and make them happen.

In the next chapter we will look at how you can boost your self esteem so that you can stop worrying about what others think about you...

Boosting
Your Self Esteem

The best way to stop worrying about what others think about you and being overly dependent on someone else is to raise your self esteem. If you are suffering with low self esteem then you will lack the motivation to change your situation. But when you see the easy tips below it will give you the chance to put a halt to the low self esteem viscous cycle.

Although the tips are easy to understand and apply, you need to accept that it is a process and will take time to see results. You need to be persistent with your efforts and you will be rewarded. So here are 12 tips to give your self esteem a much needed boost:

1. Make a List of what you have Achieved to date

Don't even think about saying that you have never achieved anything in your life. This is just your low self esteem doing the talking! All of us have accomplished more things than we give ourselves credit for.

So get out your journal or a blank sheet of paper and write down those things that you have achieved that make you feel really proud. Think about achievements at school or college, passing your driving test, helping somebody who needed it, mastering a skill etc. It doesn't matter if the achievement seems small to you – just write it down.

Spend quality time doing this and don't rush it. If you are struggling for ideas then ask your family or a friend that really knows you to help. When you have finished your list review it and wallow in the glory of your past achievements!

2. What are your Values?

Think about the true values in your life. Forget about any values that have been forced on you by others or the media. What is really important to you? The point of doing this is to check to see if you are living by your true values. Quite often people that worry about what others think do not live their lives in alignment with their true values.

If you find any discrepancies then decide what you are going to do to put this right. Record this in your journal. This is a very liberating thing to do and we urge you to do it. When you live by your true values your self esteem will go way up.

3. Get Creative

Creativity is a great way to get your juices flowing and raise your self esteem. It will stimulate your brain and you will feel so much better after performing a creative task. Again please don't say that you are not at all creative. We all have a level of creativity and you can develop this further.

So what will you do that is creative? Write a short story or a poem? Create something on your computer like a drawing or a logo? Did you used to play the piano as a child? If so then find a keyboard that you can use to create a new tune. Do anything as long as it is creative.

4. Identify Limiting Beliefs and eradicate them

This is something that will take time and effort to do for sure but you can really benefit from this so we highly recommend that you make a commitment to follow through on this. A limiting belief is something that will hold you back in life. This could be about money, your ability to do something and a number of other things.

The best way to identify limiting beliefs is to act when you have a negative thought about yourself. Rather than just accept this limitation you need to challenge it and find out where the thought came from. So if you have a thought like "you will never be able to do that" then try and identify where this comes from.

Did you hear this as a child regularly when you were growing up? Perhaps someone that had a lot of influence over you told you that you need to know your limitations and accept them? These are examples of limiting beliefs. Once you have identified them you can use techniques to replace them with empowering beliefs.

5. Get out of your Comfort Zone

One of the best ways to give your self esteem a boost is to get out of your comfort zone. What does this mean? Well we all have things that we feel comfortable doing in life. If someone asks us or you challenge yourself to do something that you have never done before then this will take you out of your comfort zone if you do it.

This can be literally anything. The reason that this works is that you will feel a great deal of satisfaction and pride achieving something that you didn't realize you could do before. It increases your confidence to go even further outside of your comfort zone.

So think of something small that you can do today. If you don't normally say hello to people that you come across in your day to day life then try smiling and saying hello politely. Or why not create a website for yourself using the free tools that are available? Choose something and then complete it. Then do something else and build your self esteem.

6. Leave the Past behind

Many people live in the past. They are haunted by mistakes that they made and this keeps their self esteem low. So make a commitment that you will stop dwelling in the past and look forward instead. If you need help from a trained counselor to achieve this then do that.

We have all made mistakes in the past and done things that we are not proud of. The best thing to do is learn from this and move on. If you feel yourself drifting back into your past then say to yourself "this has gone and I am focused on the future now". It will not be easy at first but keep persevering with this because it will set you free.

7. Provide your Help to others

In a previous section we asked you to identify your strengths and talents. Use the skills that you have to help someone else. This will give you a warm feeling inside and will do wonders for your self esteem.

Maybe you are good with children and can help others with their parenting issues. Search online for parenting forums and sign up for a couple of them – this is always free. Then find questions raised by other members of the forum and make a post offering them advice. Most people will be very grateful for this and will thank you.

Be aware that there are a small number of people on forums who are never grateful or just plain obnoxious and may respond in a negative way to your advice. If this happens then ignore them. You will find most of the members are not like this at all and will respond positively to you when you try and help.

8. Get Inspired

Instead of watching nonsense on the TV read an inspirational book or something online. There is a ton of stuff available. If you prefer to watch videos then go on YouTube and find something inspiring. You will be spoiled for choice!

The aim here is to lift you up and put you in a great frame of mind. By reading or watching something inspirational it can give you the belief that you can change your life for the better. This will make you feel a lot more positive about yourself and increase your self esteem.

9. Avoid Negative People

This can be a real tough one because you probably have close friends or family members that always see the negative in everything and will bring you down without even realizing it. If you know some of these "doom and gloom" merchants then our best advice is to avoid them as much as you can.

Try to find more positive people that you can associate with. Search online for forums or communities that have a positive vibe. Get out and about and increase your social circle by finding people with a positive outlook.

10. Make sure that you look your best

People that have low self esteem often let themselves go and stop caring about how they look. If you are in this situation then make a commitment to change and start presenting yourself to the world in a better way.

It is amazing the effect that some new clothes or a new hair style can have on you. If you are a man and have grown a beard because you couldn't be bothered then shave it off today. For women how about a new hairdo or a manicure? Take small steps to improve your appearance and improve your self esteem at the same time.

11. Tackle your Fears Head On

Do you have fears that are holding you back? Most of us have. The best way to tackle any fears that you have is to face them head on. So for example if you have a fear of public speaking then just do it anyway.

We are not suggesting that this will be easy for you. It is not easy for anyone. But if you have irrational fears then keep moving forward and face them. Will you be afraid? Yes you probably will, but you will feel so great afterwards and it will work wonders with your self esteem.

12. Treat Failure as part of your Development

For people with low self esteem, failing at something (however minor) can completely devastate them. It sends them into a totally negative spiral and there self esteem really hits rock bottom. They tell themselves that they are useless and they will always fail.

If you feel like this then we are asking you to change your thinking. We want you to accept failure as part of your growth and development. Everybody fails even though they might not want to admit it. Treat any failure as an opportunity for you to grow. You can learn why you failed and move on as a more knowledgeable individual.

Don't fear failure. Many famous peopled failed many times before they succeeded. Walt Disney was turned down by over 300 banks for his Disneyland idea. But he kept going and the rest is history. It is far better to try something and fail than be fearful and never try anything at all.

In the next chapter we will look at ways to boost your confidence if you worry about what other people think about you...

Give Your Confidence A Real Boost

People that are concerned about what others think about them often lack confidence. So by increasing your confidence you can become a lot more independent and go your own way. Having more confidence is important for everyone so if you want to increase your confidence then you will need to make a shift in your thinking.

At the end of the day it is not difficult at all to boost your confidence. But it is going to take consistent effort and a bit of time. Yes there are some techniques that will help improve your confidence almost instantly and we will cover some of these here. But for the best long lasting results be prepared to take a longer term view.

1. Change your Posture for an Instant Confidence boost

OK let's start with something really easy that will change your state and make you feel more confident straight away. If you had to walk into a room full of strangers how would you do it? Let's say that it is a party you have been invited to and you hardly know anybody.

Do you walk into the room with your head down, your shoulders rounded and with shallow breathing? This is what a lot of people with low self confidence will do. They think that if they walk around like this then nobody will want to talk to them and they can fade away into the background.

And guess what? This usually works. But why would you want to do this? It will do nothing for your confidence. Here is what you need to do instead. Change your posture so that your head is up and your shoulders are back and you are breathing normally. Add a smile to your face and then get yourself into that room.

Make eye contact with as many people as you can. This change in posture, smiling and eye contact will give you an instant confidence boost. People will naturally gravitate towards you and want to meet you and talk to you. Your self confidence will go through the roof when you change your posture in this way.

2. Think Differently

How do you think if you have made a mistake or done something to embarrass yourself? We all make mistakes and do things that are embarrassing but the way that you think about these things afterwards is critical for your confidence.

Let's look at a common moment of embarrassment for women. A woman uses the bathroom and comes out with her dress tucked into her panties. If the woman was low in confidence she would spend many nights replaying this situation over and over in her head and call herself all kinds of nasty names.

The confident woman will chuckle to herself and think "that was a bit embarrassing" and mark it down as an amusing story and get on with her life. The takeaway here is that unconfident people will over analyze a situation like this because they are so concerned about what others think of them.

Does this sound familiar?

What we recommend you do here is to stop this negative thinking cycle dead in its tracks by thinking positively. You need to break the pattern of this negative thinking so you can distract yourself with something else to take your mind away from the incident.

Is this easy to do? Yes it is but you are going to have to practice doing this quite a lot until it becomes a habit and an automatic reaction. The woman who laughed at the incident had the right approach.

Laughter is always good so if you make a mistake in the future learn to laugh about it.

3. Stop Idolizing Others

If your confidence is low it is easy to think that your flaws are much worse than other people in your social circle. The reason for this is that a lot of unconfident people idolize others by labeling them as "perfect". There is nothing wrong with using other people for inspiration as you will learn in the next chapter but you need to do it in a positive way.

There is a big difference between seeing the good in someone else and idolizing them. When you idolize someone else you are naturally going to lower your confidence so it is vital that you stop doing this because it will prevent you from moving forward with your life.

If you find yourself doing this in the future then focus on your own qualities. Think to yourself "I am very proud that I can spot good character traits in others" repeatedly so that you stop yourself going into an idolizing spiral.

4. Be Proud of who you are

If you don't like the same things as others do then that is OK. You don't have to follow all of the latest trends like others do. In fact it shows character that some of the meaningless trends that a lot of people follow these days do not sway you.

It really doesn't matter that your friends all like a certain type of music and you prefer something else. You need to accept that you are happy and stay true to yourself. Write a list of things that you like and dislike in your journal and get comfortable with your choices.

In the next chapter we will reveal some advanced tactics for comparing yourself to others in a healthy way...

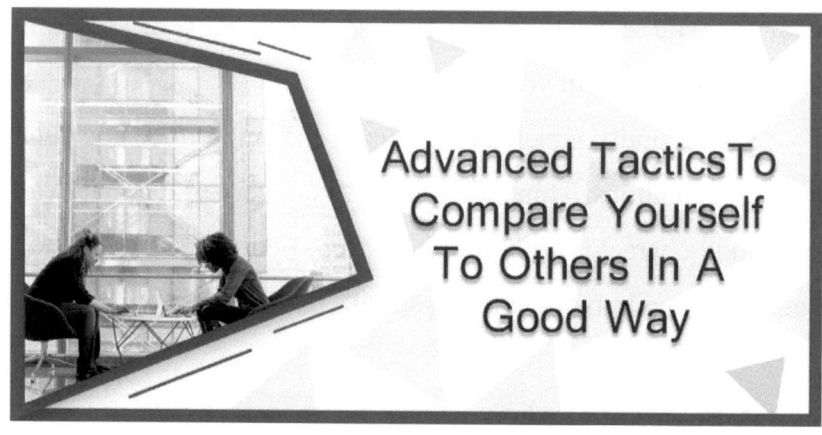

Advanced TacticsTo
Compare Yourself
To Others In A
Good Way

You already know that comparing yourself to other people is a natural thing to do. In this chapter we will discuss how you can make comparisons that are beneficial to you rather than evoke feelings of negativity. So let's take a look at the best ways to do this.

1. What are your Motivations for the Comparison?

To make healthy comparisons you need the right intent. Otherwise you can find yourself at the mercy of unhealthy comparisons. If you don't have the right motivation for a comparison then it is better to not compare yourself at all.

If you admire someone that has achieved what you want to achieve then your intent needs to be to identify the gap between you in terms of knowledge and experience. You can then use this to plan your next moves. Ignore everything else about the person and just use this information to drive your life forward.

2. Be really Curious about this Experience and Knowledge Gap

Once you have identified the gap between you and the successful person you need to ramp up your curiosity so that you find out every little detail about what you are missing. This requires a deep dive into what the person does and how they have achieved their success.

Ask yourself a number of questions about the gap. If you cannot find the answers that you need then be brave and reach out to the person that you are comparing yourself to. Ask them specific questions about how they got to where they are today. Most people like to tell their story and will probably be willing to help you.

3. Do it Your Way

Always remember that you are not trying to become the person that you are comparing yourself to. What you are looking for is similar results. You are very different to everyone else and will approach things differently to them. It is essential that you embrace these differences and do things your way.

Whatever you need to do to bridge the experience and knowledge gap between you and the other person has to be done your way. This is the fastest way to success for you. You can then look back and be proud of the fact that it was all your own work.

4. Be Prepared to make the Effort

If you really want to achieve similar results to the person who you are comparing yourself to then you need to be prepared to put in consistent effort. There is no magic button to press here. Don't think that you cannot achieve what they have. It just takes a lot of hard work on your part. They are human the same as you.

When you develop a work ethic it will drive you to success. Hard work is a term that most people have difficulty with these days but never take this attitude. Having to work hard to achieve something is a lot more satisfying than having something that you achieved easily.

In the final chapter we will share with you the best practices for comparing yourself with others...

Comparing
Yourself With Others
Best Practices

You have learned a great deal reading this book. To help you to move forward in the best possible way we have 7 best practices for you that we strongly recommend that you follow. So let's get into it:

1. Always use Comparisons to Improve yourself

You can derive a lot of benefit by using comparisons with others to improve yourself. To do this successfully you need to be clear on your intent and motivation. When you do this right it can provide you with a great inspirational boost.

2. Never use Comparisons to Validate how good you are

A lot of people will use comparisons with others to validate the fact that they are superior to them in some way. This is a very unhealthy comparison which is likely to have a lot of negative consequences.

3. Don't Compare yourself to others based on Insecurity and Fear

This is the worse form of comparison which can lead to intense anger and bitterness. Unfortunately it is the most common form of comparison and if you are doing this now then you need to use the techniques in this guide to stop doing this.

4. Compare yourself with yourself

Get into the habit of focusing on yourself and monitoring your own progress. Rather than compare yourself to others use self comparison instead. Set yourself goals and check your progress against them regularly.

5. Do it your way

Accept the fact that you are different to everyone else. What works for some people may not work for you and vice versa. It is essential that you do things your way. Learn from others but create your own plan and do your own thing.

6. Learn to Love yourself

Get over any hang-ups you have about loving yourself. Self love is very empowering and will help you to become more confident in yourself and reduce the need to compare yourself with others. Being over dependent on others is very unhealthy and you need to take action to move away from this as soon as you can.

7. Boost your Self Esteem and Confidence

When you have a high self esteem and confidence you will not need to compare yourself with others very much if at all. Start a journal and make entries every day about the progress you are making. Look back over past achievements and challenges to see how far you have come. Work every day on boosting your self esteem and increasing your confidence.

Conclusion

Congratulations you now know why people compare themselves to others and how you can avoid negative comparisons and use positive comparisons to make a big difference to your life. We have worked hard to bring you this comprehensive guide and to provide you with all of the information that you need to make a positive transition.

Living as life where you are constantly worried about what others think about you is not recommended. You will find that people are controlling your life and that you can never be truly happy without their approval.

So we urge you to take what you have learned in this guide and put it into action. Please don't just read this guide and then do nothing. Your situation will not change for the better unless you act on what you have learned.

We wish you every success making the move to positive comparisons with others and freeing yourself from the worry about what others think about you.

Printed by Libri Plureos GmbH in Hamburg,
Germany